Read and Do Science

DIRTY and CLEAN

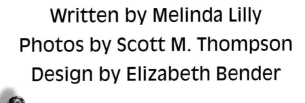

Written by Melinda Lilly
Photos by Scott M. Thompson
Design by Elizabeth Bender

Educational Consultants

Kimberly Weiner, Ed.D

Betty Carter, Ed.D

Maria Czech, Ph.D
California State University Northridge

Rourke

Publishing LLC

Vero Beach, Florida 32963

Before You Read This Book

Think about these facts:

1. Why do you wash your hands before you eat?
2. Why do you put food in the refrigerator?

The experiments in this book should be undertaken with adult supervision.

The photo on page 23 is courtesy of the National Park Service.

Library of Congress Cataloging-in-Publication Data

ISBN 1-58952-636-8

Printed in the USA

Table of Contents

Dirt shows up in different ways. There's dust under the rug, mud by a pond, and more.

What happens to food that gets dirty?

Clean your hands with a wipe. Clean half of the apple or potato by wiping it.

Put it inside the baggie and seal it.

Not that kind of seal! Close up the bag.

6

Label the bag with the word, "Clean," and the date.

Dip the other half of the apple or potato into the dirt.

Ewww, lucky you!

7

Seal it inside a baggie.

Label it "Dirty," and mark the date.

WARNING: Keep the bags closed! Smelling or breathing air with **mold** can be harmful.

It's alive!

Check the baggies in four days. Is the dirty food beginning to **decay,** or rot?

Why does icky stuff start growing on the dirty food first? **Germs** and mold like dirt. When you wash or use a wet wipe, you remove dirt.

9

Why Not Make the Germs Happy (and Dirty)?

Germs are too tiny to see, but they pack a wallop! Some of them make people sick. That's why it's important to keep clean.

I HAB A CODE ID BY DOSE.

(He means he has a cold in his nose.)

Check the bags again in four days. How did mold get inside the sealed bag?

Mold grows from tiny **spores,** or seeds. When you first opened the bag, spores entered along with the food, air, and dirt. They settled on the food.

Hungry Yet?

Mold helps make food go rotten by oozing **chemicals.** Rotten food is yummy to mold. Mold eats rotten food.

Check the bags one week later. The mold is having a feast!

Want some?

How Are You Like the Clean Food?

Notice how the peel, or skin, of the clean food did not decay. One of the jobs of skin is to keep out germs. You help your skin by washing often.

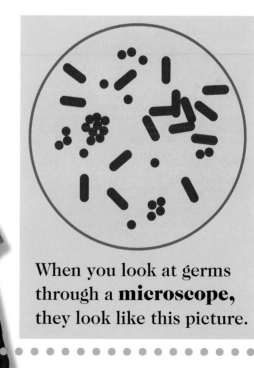

When you look at germs through a **microscope,** they look like this picture.

Dirty Money, Clean Coins

When you are dirty, you wash and become clean. However, sometimes you need more than soap to get things clean.

Mold used chemicals to rot the apple. You can use a **chemical reaction** to clean a penny!

Hmmm . . . why do copper pennies turn brown?

The **copper** in pennies changes because of air, not because of dirt. **Oxygen** in the air reacts with the copper. That results in **copper oxide,** the brown color on a penny.

Make your pennies clean again!

Pretty Pennies

What You Need:
- Dirty pennies
- 2 cups white vinegar
- 1/4 cup salt
- A bowl
- Water
- Paper towels
- A clock

I'll help!

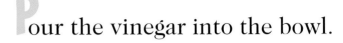

Pour the vinegar into the bowl.

Add the salt.

Drop in the pennies.
Swirl them around.

17

Are the pennies brighter? Take out the pennies after five minutes.

This one's not brighter. Find out why on page 23.

Wash the pennies and your hands.

Now I'm a pretty penny!

Why Are the Pennies Clean?

Vinegar and salt mix with the copper oxide that makes the pennies brown. The mix of vinegar and salt **dissolves,** or cleans away, the copper oxide.

Thanks!

Thanks to a chemical reaction, the pennies are clean . . . for now.

Find out why this penny is green! Save the vinegar bath and turn to page 23 after reading.

Down and Dirty

Why can't you watch copper and oxygen mix when they make copper oxide? Like germs settling on the apple, the mixing is too small to see without a microscope.

It can be hard to see how something comes clean or why you shouldn't eat a mud pie. It's easy to see how fun it is to play with dirty and clean!

microscope

Glossary

chemical reaction (KEM ih kul ree AK shun) — when chemicals mix and cause a change in each other

chemicals (KEM ih kulz) — substances that can cause a change in things and have a certain make-up

chlorine (KLOR een) — a chemical found in salt and used for cleaning

copper (KOP ur) — a reddish-brown metal

copper oxide (KOP ur OK sied) — copper and oxygen mixed

decay (dih KAY) — rot

dissolve (dih ZOLV) — to melt and break up

germs (JURMZ) — very small living things that can cause illness

microscope (MY kroh skoap) — a scientific tool that makes tiny things able to be seen

mold (MOLD) — a growth that forms on animals or plants and helps decay

oxygen (OK see jun) — a gas that that is necessary in breathing

spores (SPORZ) — seeds or germs

Take It Further: A Penny for Your Thoughts

1. Put the pennies back into the vinegar and salt bath.

2. Do not rinse them when you take them out.

3. Wait an hour. Look at the pennies.

Why did they turn green? Salt includes the chemical **chlorine** in it. It's the chemical used to clean pools. Chlorine mixed with copper and oxygen. The combination turned the pennies green!

Think About It!

1. If you let the food continue to rot, what would eventually happen to it?
2. The Statue of Liberty is made of copper. Why is it green?
3. Put these actions in the right order:

   _____ An apple falls off the tree.

   _____ Mold grows on the old apple where the skin is broken.

   _____ A bird tears the skin of the apple when it takes a bite.

   _____ The apple decays into the soil.

Index